Smoke

by Lilly Cho
illustrated by Kristen Goeters

Practice Decodable 55

McGraw Hill Education

Bothell, WA • Chicago, IL • Columbus, OH • New York, NY

MHEonline.com

Send all inquiries to:
McGraw-Hill Education
8787 Orion Place
Columbus, OH 43240

ISBN: 978-0-02-133454-4
MHID: 0-02-133454-4

Printed in China.

8 9 10 11 12 DSS 27 26 25 24 23

Matt's nose told him of a problem. He smelled smoke. It was close.

Matt looked down the block.

Smoke rose over Mr. Jones's home.

Matt made a quick call.
He hoped for fast help. Go! Go!

Sirens blared, and trucks arrived.
Hoses filled the block.

In a short time, the problem was over.
"Thanks, Matt," said Mr. Jones.

"It was not a problem," said Matt. "Thank this nose!"